ATTENTION

This book comes with a cassette tape. This tape is necessary to complete several chapters in the book.

Please send a photocopy of your receipt of purchase to Metamorphous Press and we will send the cassette tape first class mail.

Mail to:
METAMORPHOUS PRESS
P.O. Box 10616
Portland, Oregon 97210-0616

Name _____

Address _____

City _____ State _____ Zip _____

1
D1502591

Basic Techniques

Book I

by

Linnaea Marvell-Mell

Metamorphous Press
Portland, OR

Published by

Metamorphous Press
P.O. Box 10616
Portland, OR 97210

ISBN 1-55552-016-2

DEDICATION

This book is dedicated to all those
like myself who have waded the muddy
waters

ACKNOWLEDGEMENTS

I wish to express my admiration and gratitude to John Grinder, Richard Bandler, Leslie Cameron-Bandler and all those members of the original research team who had the courage, the wisdom, and the audacity to develop the stuff of Neuro-Linguistic Programming.

My special thanks go to Susan Marcus for introducing me to the concepts, and for her role as mentor.

My deepest appreciation goes to Byron Lewis for his role as teacher and for his continued assistance in helping me to refine the content of these workbooks.

And last but not least, I want to thank my husband Wayne Mell, my children Loren, Jared and Jaime and my friend Paul Roberge for their continued support and encouragement as I undertook this project.

Linnaea Marvell-Mell

CONTENTS

INTRODUCTION

The purpose of this workbook is to acquaint the reader more intimately with the skills necessary for the successful utilization of Neuro-Linguistic Programming techniques.

Before I go on I would like to tell you about a friend of mine who is a successful author. I have long admired this woman for her ability to produce quality works year after year seemingly without being disrupted by outside influences. So it was with great surprise that I listened to her tell the following story.

It seems that my friend was invited to join a select group of people who were also well published authors. This group would meet for several weeks and share their approaches to writing. My friend was most excited by the prospect and went to the meetings in eager anticipation.

What most pleased my friend was that the group included a person whose works she had recently come to admire. To her this individual seemed a veritable master of the craft. So she went and listened attentively to everything he had to say. His words were inspiring to her and she came home eager to put into practice everything she had learned.

At first she was able to use what she had learned and was proud of her efforts, but when she went to re-read her newly completed story it was strange to her and she was dissatisfied with it. Most of all she feared how others would react to her changed style. Since she already knew that her old way of doing things worked for her, it was easy to slip back into the old ways and to forget the enthusiasm she had brought back with her from the meetings.

Then one day she received a phone call from the man she had so admired. As they talked, her enthusiasm renewed itself. During the conversation he mentioned that he had just switched his car from gasoline to gasohol and that his car wasn't running very well. My friend, in turn, shared her own similar experience. And it was with great pride that she was able to tell him her solution to the problem. She had found that her car was much better able to make the adjustment when she began by mixing only small amounts at a time with the gasoline. Eventually, she was able to add greater and greater quantities of the new fuel, until the car ran as smoothly with the mix as it had with the gasoline alone.

The person was delighted with the information and my friend was happy to have shared something with a man from whom she had learned so much. They finished talking about their writing and even arranged to meet in the future. When she went back to her typewriter, my friend was especially pleased to find that she was able to use some of the things she had learned at the meetings many months before.

I was pleased to hear this story and to know that a woman I had thought did so well to begin with was still growing in her work.

As I was saying, this workbook was written to assist those newly introduced to NLP techniques in developing more sophisticated skills. Each exercise has been planned so that it builds on skills developed through the previous exercises. Most people will be using the workbook along with either a text on the subject or in conjunction with a workshop. **Basic Techniques in NLP** is also an excellent tool for use as a follow-up to training in the field. At the beginning of each section you will find references to sources that we believe best present the pertinent content information.

This workbook will help you to determine those areas in which you are already competent and those in which you want to develop more skills. If you find that you have difficulty with any of the exercises, you may want to repeat them several times until they are easier for you. The instructions for each exercise will be given on a separate page from the forms for the responses. Several copies of each response sheet will follow the instructions so that the exercise can be repeated if you wish.

Competency in the basic skills takes time and practice. Give yourself time to process what you have learned.

NEURO-LINGUISTIC PROGRAMMING

People often act as though their experience of reality were the same as reality itself. However, the parameters of human experience are fixed by the limited capacity of the sensory receptors to accurately perceive the real world. So man's experience of reality can never be precisely the same as reality. The sensory organs act as a set of filters translating external experience into limited internal experience.

Human beings may enrich their understanding of reality by externally modeling internal experience through language. Thus multiple internal experiences can be shared. However, the parameters of human communication are fixed by the limited capacity of the language to accurately represent internal experience. So language acts as a set of filters translating internal experience into limited external representation. Thus one human being can no more be sure that his/her internal experience matches that of another than (s)he can be sure of his/her ability to accurately perceive external reality. It is hardly surprising, then, that human beings are often frustrated in their attempts to communicate with one another or to make sense out of the "real" world.

The sensory receptors and language act as filters for human experience. Communication difficulties often arise when an individual is limited from making full use of either his/her sensory facilities or his/her linguistic representations of experience. Communication may be further inhibited when the processes for modeling reality or the experience of it are not shared by two or more people — as when people do not share the same language.

The processes by which human beings filter their experience through their senses and through language are of special interest to the communicator. Neuro-Linguistic Programmng is the study of these filtering processes. The field of Neuro-Linguistic Programming offers the communicator a set of explicit tools for understanding and utilizing these processes. In other words it is a working model of the human modeling processes — a meta model.

Human beings strive to make sense out of their experience in any way they can, so that even two individuals without a common language will find ways to communicate. So, with or without language, human beings use non-verbal means for communicating as well (i.e. sounds, gestures, expressions, smells, tastes, etc.). Non-verbal (analog) communciation may enrich the process of modeling experience, but is still not the same as experience itself.

Since human beings have differing internal experiences in response to reality, their external expressions may differ as well. Here again, accurate communciation is confounded by the differing expressions. Neuro-Linguistic Programming seeks to understand the human modeling processes as they are expressed through sensory perception, language and analog communications.

The communicator, through the techniques of Neuro-Linguistic Programming, becomes aware of the similarities and differences between his/her model of the world and that of person(s) with whom (s)he is communicating. These tools offer the individual methods for expanding his/her own modeling processes, they provide the means for assisting others in enriching impoverished models of reality, and they facilitate the ability of individuals to more accurately share their models of the world. Human interaction will always be subject to the constraints of the filters through which it operates, but the field of Neuro-Linguistic Programming offers human beings the opportunity to minimize the personal and public effects of those constraints.

ACCESSING CUES

The exercises in this section have been designed to help you sharpen your ability to recognize accessing cues and to increase your flexibility in this area.

ACCESSING CUES: SOURCE MATERIAL

1 **Magic of NLP Demystified,** Lewis and Pucelik, Metamorphous Press, 1982; pp. 115-128.

2 **Frogs Into Princes,** Bandler and Grinder, Real People
   Press, 1979; pp. 19-27.

ACCESSING CUES: CONTENT REVIEW

1. Define:
   a. Eidetic Images _____
   b. Constructed Images _____
   c. Internal Dialogue _____
   d. Internally Generated Stimuli _____
   _____
   e. Lead System _____
   f. Occular Accessing Cues _____
   g. Pupil Response _____
   h. Reversed Accessing Cues _____
2. How can you identify people's accessing cues when their eyes are closed?
   _____
3. The "telephone posture" indicates what kind of accessing? _____
   _____
4. When are you most likely to find reversed accessing cues? _____
   _____
5. Is the information people "access" always in their conscious awareness?
   _____
6. In response to the question, "What did you do last night?", the person flares
   his/her nostrils and closes his/her eyes. This is an example of _____
   _____ accessing.
7. Give an example of where accessing cues are important._____
   _____
   _____

CODE FOR EXERCISES 1, 2, & 3

V^c - VISUALLY CONSTRUCTED
V^r - VISUALLY REMEMBERED
A^c - AUDITORY CONSTRUCTED
A^r - AUDITORY REMEMBERED
A^i - AUDITORY INTERNAL DIALOGUE
K   - KINESTHETIC

EXERCISE #1
ELICITING ACCESSING CUES

INSTRUCTIONS

On the following page is a set of questions you might use to determine a person's eye movement patterns (accessing cues). Use the content of the questions to determine which representational system the respondent would use if you asked the question. Enter your answer in the space provided using the code on the previous page.

EXAMPLE:

"Can you tell me, without looking, what color shoes you are wearing?", would require that the respondent use a visually remembered (Vr) eye movement.

Note: The eye movements have been pictured for you as a hint.

EXERCISE #1
ELICITING ACCESSING CUES
RESPONSES

QUESTIONS	EYE MOVEMENT	SYSTEM
What color was your mother's hair when you last saw her?		
What would your Mother look like with green hair?		
Can you recall the tune to your favorite song?		
What would that song sound like with church bells in the background?		
What does snow feel like?		
What are you telling yourself right now?		

EXERCISE #1
ELICITING ACCESSING CUES
RESPONSES

QUESTIONS	EYE MOVEMENT	SYSTEM
What color was your mother's hair when you last saw her?		
What would your Mother look like with green hair?		
Can you recall the tune to your favorite song?		
What would that song sound like with church bells in the background?		
What does snow feel like?		
What are you telling yourself right now?		

Exercise #2 Cont'd

13._____14._____15._____ 16. _____

17._____18._____19._____ 20. _____

21._____22._____23._____24. _____

Exercise #2 Cont'd

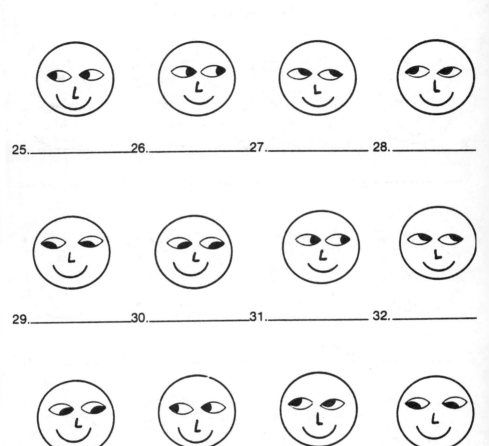

25._____ 26._____ 27._____ 28._____

29._____ 30._____ 31._____ 32._____

33._____ 34._____ 35._____ 36._____

EXERCISE #2 — OBSERVING ACCESSING CUES

RESPONSES

1._____ 2._____ 3._____ 4._____

5._____ 6._____ 7._____ 8._____

9._____ 10._____ 11._____ 12._____

Exercise #2 Cont'd

13._____14._____15._____ 16._____

17._____18._____19._____ 20._____

21._____22._____23._____ 24._____

Exercise #2 Cont'd

25._____ 26._____ 27._____ 28. _____

29._____ 30._____ 31._____ 32. _____

33._____ 34._____ 35._____ 36. _____

EXERCISE #3
OBSERVING
ACCESSING CUES—2

INSTRUCTIONS

This exercise is the same as the exercise you just completed except that the pictures are of real people. Look at the eyes of the people in the following pictures. Determine which representational system each individual is using. Enter your answers in the space beneath each picture using the code.

EXAMPLE:

A^i

Note: You may wish to repeat this exercise and go through it faster than is comfortable for you.

EXERCISE #3 — OBSERVING ACCESSING CUES

RESPONSES

  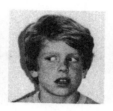

1._____ 2._____ 3._____ 4._____

5._____ 6._____ 7._____ 8._____

9._____ 10._____ 11._____ 12._____

17

Exercise #3 Cont'd

 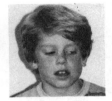  

13._____ 14._____ 15._____ 16._____

  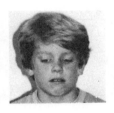 

17._____ 18._____ 19._____ 20._____

21._____ 22._____ 23._____ 24._____

EXERCISE #3 — OBSERVING ACCESSING CUES

RESPONSES

1._____ 2._____ 3._____ 4._____

 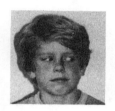  

5._____ 6._____ 7._____ 8._____

9._____10._____11._____12._____

Exercise #3 Cont'd

 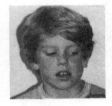  

13._____ 14._____ 15._____ 16._____

17._____ 18._____ 19._____ 20._____

21._____ 22._____ 23._____ 24._____

SUGGESTED EXERCISES
ACCESSING CUES

GROUP EXERCISE

Participants: Person A - observes
Person B - accesses

Procedure:
"A" and "B" face one another. "A" asks "B" questions (such as those in exercise #1) that presuppose "B" must access a specific system in order to respond. "A" maps "B's" accessing schematic. "A" should elicit the responses as naturally as possible and may need to ask several questions to get the appropriate response from "B". The more difficult the question the more likely "A" will get an accurate response. It may be important to differentiate a person's lead system from other accessing cues.

INDIVIDUAL EXERCISE

Procedure:
Sit in front of the television set, close enough to reach the volume control easily. During a live show (such as a talk show) observe, with the volume control turned down, the movements of a speaker's eyes. Use the volume control to check the person's predicates. Notice when they match the accessing patterns. Notice when they don't. Make mental note of the accessing schematic the individual is using.

CALIBRATION

The exercises in this section have been designed to help you sharpen your ability to calibrate quickly and accurately.

CALIBRATION: SOURCE MATERIAL

1   **Therapeutic Metaphors**, Gordon, Meta Publications, 1979, pp 165-166.

2   **Transformations**, Bandler and Grinder, Real People Press, 1981; pp. 201-212.

CALIBRATION CONTENT REVIEW

1. Define:
   a. Calibration _____

   b. Minimal Cues _____

   c. Analog _____

   d. Calibrated Communication _____

   _____

   e. Subliminal Cues _____

2. You know when you have calibrated to an individual when _____

   _____

3. Name three situations in which the process of calibration can be useful.__

   _____

4. Calibration is one way to demystify the apparent "mind reading" done by us all
   upon occasion. True or False

5. Calibration utilizes immediately verifiable sensory grounded experience to
   identify a person's _____ .

EXERCISE #4
AUDITORY CALIBRATION

INSTRUCTIONS

PART ONE

For this exercise use the tape. You will hear a person give descriptions of seven different experiences. Each experience will be identified as one of the following internal states: **sadness, happiness, pleasure, anger, defensiveness, excitement, openness to learning.** In the spaces provided under Part I, record the key phrases and tonalities in such a way that you will recognize them when you hear them again.

EXAMPLE:

SADNESS: *"I just felt so sorry"* (voice labored, emphasize just and soooo).

PART TWO

You will now hear the same speaker describe twenty-one different experiences. Listen for the key phrases and tonalities that you heard in Part I and identify the state of the speaker as **sadness, happiness, pleasure, anger, defensiveness, excitement, or openness to learning.** Record your answers in the spaces provided under Part II.

EXAMPLE:

You hear "I just felt so sorry" said the same way you heard it in Part I. You identify the internal state of the speaker as *sadness.*

EXERCISE #4   AUDITORY CALIBRATION

RESPONSES

PART ONE

KEY PHRASES AND TONALITIES

Sadness _____

Happiness _____

Pleasure _____

Anger _____

Defensiveness _____

Excitement _____

Openness to learning _____

PART TWO

1._____	8._____	15._____
2._____	9._____	16._____
3._____	10._____	17._____
4._____	11._____	18._____
5._____	12._____	19._____
6._____	13._____	20._____
7._____	14._____	21._____

EXERCISE #4 AUDITORY CALIBRATION

RESPONSES

PART ONE

KEY PHRASES AND TONALITIES

Sadness_____

Happiness_____

Pleasure _____

Anger_____

Defensiveness _____

Excitement _____

Openness to learning _____

PART TWO

1._____ 8._____15. _____

2._____ 9._____16. _____

3._____10._____17. _____

4._____11._____18. _____

5._____12._____19. _____

6._____13._____20. _____

7._____14._____21. _____

EXERCISE #5   VISUAL CALIBRATION

INSTRUCTIONS

Study each of the following pictures. Each picture shows a person experiencing one of the internal states described in the previous exercise: sadness, happiness, pleasure. anger, defensiveness. excitement, openness to learning. Take as long as you need to calibrate to the individual's facial expressions.

EXCITEMENT

OPENNESS TO LEARNING

DEFENSIVENESS

SADNESS

HAPPINESS

PLEASURE

ANGER

In each of the pictures on the following pages, the individual will express one of the internal states you studied on the previous page. Identify the internal state of the person as either: **openness to learning, defensiveness, excitement, sadness, happiness, pleasure or anger.** Indicate your responses in the spaces beneath each picture.

EXAMPLE:

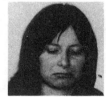
Sadness

Note: You may wish to repeat this exercise until you can do it quickly.

EXERCISE #5 — VISUAL CALIBRATION

RESPONSES

  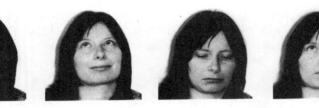 

1._____ 2._____ 3._____ 4. ._____

  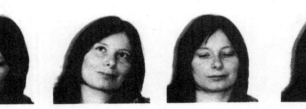 

5._____ 6._____ 7._____ 8. _____

  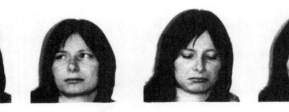 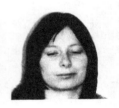

9._____10._____11._____ 12. _____

Exercise #5 Cont'd

   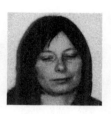

13. _Anger_   14. _Open to learning_ 15. _Excitement_   16. _Pleasure_

17. _Happiness_   18. _Defensiveness_ 19. _Sadness_   20. _Excitement_

21. _Anger_   22. _Pleasure_   23. Defensiveness 24. _Happiness_

EXERCISE #5 — VISUAL CALIBRATION

RESPONSES

1._____ 2._____ 3._____ 4._____

5._____ 6._____ 7._____ 8._____

9._____ 10._____ 11._____ 12._____

Exercise #5 Cont'd

13._____ 14._____ 15._____ 16._____

17._____ 18._____ 19._____ 20._____

 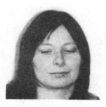  

21._____ 22._____ 23._____ 24._____

SUGGESTED EXERCISES
CALIBRATION

GROUP EXERCISE

Participants: Person A - observer
Person B - experiencer

Procedure:
"A" and "B" face one another. "B" remembers some (personally identified) positive experience. "B" should "get into" the experience fully (i.e. see, hear, feel, taste, and smell the event as if re-experiencing it).

"A" calibrates to the positive experience. Jot down any minimal cues such as breathing, muscle tone, accessing patterns, flush of skin, lower lip size, posture, etc. that may be used to identify this particular internal state the next time "B" experiences it.

Repeat this procedure with a "negative" experience. Test for accurate calibration by having "B" remember either the negative or positive experience again without indentifying the memory for "A". "A" then identifies "B's" internal state as either positive or negative based on the previous calibrations. Repeat until "A" can successfully identify "B's" internal state in three out of four trials. "A" and "B" switch roles.

INDIVIDUAL EXERCISE

Procedure:
Watch a live talk show on television. Calibrate to a particular internal state of one of the guests. Turn down the volume and watch for the minimal cues that indicate a return to the same internal state. Turn up the volume to "check", using the content of the conversation as a measure of your accuracy.

PACING AND LEADING

These exercises have been designed to help you sharpen your ability to both pace and lead.

PACING AND LEADING:
SOURCE MATERIAL

1 **Magic of NLP Demystified,** Lewis and Pucelik, Metamorphous Press, 1982; pp. 115-128.

2 **TRANCE-Formations,** Bandler and Grinder, Real People Press, 1981; pp. 34-43.

3 **Neuro-Linguistic Programming, Vol. I,** Dilts, Grinder, Bandler, Bandler, and DeLozier, Meta Publications, 1980; pp. 107-119.

PACING AND LEADING
CONTENT REVIEW

1. Define:
   a. Pacing _____
   b. Leading _____
   c. Mirroring _____
   d. Rapport _____
   e. Predicates_____
   f. Representational Systems_____

   _____
   g. Predicate Preference _____

   _____

2. The word "understand" presupposes which representational system? ___

   _____

3. A person says in a monotone with arms folded over the chest, "I know what the potentialities are." This person is operating from which representational system?_____

   _____

4. You might expect a person who operates consistently from his/her emotions and feelings to use _____predicates.

5. What is meant by the axiom, "pacing and leading are self-prescriptive?"___

   _____

6. What are the primary ways of representing our experience?_____

   _____

7. How can a person's language indicate how (s)he makes sense of the world?
   _____

8. What is the difference between a person's lead system and his/her preferred representational system?_____
   _____

9. Give an example of mirroring in each of the following representational systems:
   VISUAL _____
   AUDITORY _____
   KINESTHETIC _____
   DIGITAL _____

EXERCISE #6
HEARING PREDICATES

INSTRUCTIONS

For this exercise use the tape. As you listen to the story, record every predicate you hear that is indicative of a representational system. If necessary, stop the tape so that you will have time to record your answers. Record your answers on the next page.

EXAMPLE:

You hear: "**The light green shades of the trees seemed dim against the deep blue sky.**"

You list the following predicates:

> **light green shades**
> **seemed**
> **dim**
> **deep blue**

EXERCISE #6   HEARING PREDICATES

RESPONSES

PREDICATES LIST:

EXERCISE #6   HEARING PREDICATES

RESPONSES

PREDICATES LIST:

EXERCISE #7
PACING REPRESENTATIONAL SYSTEMS

INSTRUCTIONS

PART A

For this exercise listen again to the section of the tape you used for exercise #6. This time as you hear each predicate, identify the representational system with which that predicate goes. Record your reponse in column A on the next page.

EXAMPLE:

You hear the predicates **dim** and **seemed**. You would record these under the visual column A:

VISUAL	
A	B
dim	
seemed	

PART B

Now go back and look at each predicate you have written. You may also listen to the tape or say the predicate to yourself. As you do any or all of these things, think of a similar word in the same representational system. Record your answer in column B.

EXAMPLE:

VISUAL	
A	B
dim	faded
seemed	appeared

EXERCISE #7
PACING REPRESENTATIONAL SYSTEMS

RESPONSES

VISUAL		KINESTHETIC		AUDITORY	
A	B	A	B	A	B

EXERCISE #7
PACING REPRESENTATIONAL SYSTEMS

RESPONSES

AUDITORY DIGITAL		OLFACTORY GUSTATORY	
A	B	A	B

EXERCISE #7
PACING REPRESENTATIONAL SYSTEMS

RESPONSES

VISUAL		KINESTHETIC		AUDITORY	
A	B	A	B	A	B

EXERCISE #7
PACING REPRESENTATIONAL SYSTEMS

RESPONSES

AUDITORY DIGITAL		OLFACTORY GUSTATORY	
A	B	A	B

EXERCISE #8
PACING BREATHING

INSTRUCTIONS

For this exercise use the tape. As you listen, you will be given suggestions for pacing your breathing to the speaker's pauses. Follow the instructions on the tape and pay attention to any changes in your internal experience as you change your breathing. When you have finished, describe what you did on the following page, including any changes in your internal experience.

EXAMPLE:

"When I speeded up my breathing, I had to breathe higher in my chest to keep up with the pace. It seemed to me that I was gasping and a little out of control."

EXERCISE #8   PACING BREATHING

RESPONSES

Description of your breathing changes and changes in your internal experience while pacing breathing:

EXERCISE #8 PACING BREATHING

RESPONSES

Description of your breathing changes and changes in your internal experience while pacing breathing:

EXERCISE #9
HEARING VOICE CHANGES

INSTRUCTIONS

Listen again to the section of the tape you used for exercises six and seven. As you listen, become aware of any changes in voice tonality. Code your answers in the spaces on the next page as follows:

CODE

PITCH RISES	↑	BREATHINESS	B
PITCH LOWERS	↓	NASAL	N
FAST TEMPO	F	CHESTY	C
MODERATE TEMPO	M	LOUDER	L
SLOW TEMPO	S	SOFTER	Q

EXAMPLE:

_↑QC___ / ___S↓B___ / ___↑N___ / ___F↑B___ / ___LF↓___ / ___↑M_____ /

NOTE: There are no right or wrong answers. Allow yourself to play with other kinds of changes that you can identify as well as those above.

EXERCISE #9   HEARING VOICE CHANGES

RESPONSES

_____/ _____/ _____/ _____/ _____/ _____/

_____/ _____/ _____/ _____/ _____/ _____/

_____/ _____/ _____/ _____/ _____/ _____/

_____/ _____/ _____/ _____/ _____/ _____/

_____/ _____/ _____/ _____/ _____/ _____/

_____/ _____/ _____/ _____/ _____/ _____/

EXERCISE #9   HEARING VOICE CHANGES

RESPONSES

_____/ _____/ _____/ _____/ _____/ _____

_____/ _____/ _____/ _____/ _____/ _____

_____/ _____/ _____/ _____/ _____/ _____

_____/ _____/ _____/ _____/ _____/ _____

_____/ _____/ _____/ _____/ _____/ _____

_____/ _____/ _____/ _____/ _____/ _____

EXERCISE #10
MIRRORING

INSTRUCTIONS

While at home, at work, or in any other setting where you are around other people, engage a person in conversation. Without telling them what you are doing, mold your own body into a position that mirrors that of the other person. After you have done this for a while, begin also mirroring any hand or arm gestures the person has used frequently. When you have finished, describe what happened and the results in the spaces on the next page.

EXAMPLE:

Postures other party uses: *head resting on hand, legs crossed*

Postures you mirrored: *both of above*

Results: *the other person had been disagreeing with me, he began to agree with some of the things I was saying*

Gestures other party used: *rubbed nose a lot, scratched head & eye*

Gestures you mirrored: *rubbing nose*

Results: *he began to laugh*

NOTE: Mirroring another person's behavior is one form of pacing.

EXERCISE #10 — MIRRORING

RESPONSES

Postures other party used: _____
_____
_____

Postures you mirrored: _____
_____
_____

Results: _____
_____
_____

Gestures other party used: _____
_____
_____

Gestures you mirrored: _____
_____
_____

Results: _____
_____
_____
_____

EXERCISE #10 — MIRRORING

RESPONSES

Postures other party used: _____
_____
_____

Postures you mirrored: _____
_____
_____

Results: _____
_____
_____

Gestures other party used: _____
_____
_____

Gestures you mirrored: _____
_____
Results: _____
_____
_____
_____

BEHAVIORS LIST FOR EXERCISES 11-14

EYE MOVEMENTS
PREDICATES
BREATHING
VOICE TONALITIES
FACIAL EXPRESSIONS
KEY PHRASES AND TONALITIES
BODY POSTURE AND MOVEMENTS

EXERCISE #11
PACING

INSTRUCTIONS

Pick a behavior from the list on the previous page. Observe the way some other person uses that behavior. Match the behavior with your own. Be aware of what happens as a "result" of what you are doing. Record the results on the next page.

EXAMPLE:

#1 You are talking with someone and you hear that most of the predictes they are using are visual. *You respond to them by using predicates that are also from the visual system.*

#2 As you are talking with another person, you observe that their breathing is mostly slow and deep in the chest. *You match your breathing to theirs.*

EXERCISE #11 — PACING

RESPONSES

Behavior you chose to observe: _____
_____
_____

How the other person exhibited the behavior: _____
_____
_____

How you paced the behavior: _____
_____
_____

Results: _____
_____
_____

EXERCISE #11 — PACING

RESPONSES

behavior you chose to observe: _____
_____
_____

How the other person exhibited the behavior: _____
_____
_____

How you paced the behavior: _____
_____
_____

Results: _____
_____
_____

EXERCISE #12
CROSS-OVER MIRRORING

INSTRUCTIONS

Pick a behavior from the list. Observe the way another person uses the behavior. Pick another behavior from the list. Use this second behavior to pace the first behavior. Record the results on the next page.

EXAMPLE:

Observe how the other person is breathing. *You use the movement of your index finger to pace the rhythm of the other person's breathing.*

NOTE: Pacing one behavior with another is called cross-over mirroring.

EXERCISE #12 — CROSS OVER MIRRORING

RESPONSES

Behavior the other person used: _____
_____
_____

Behavior you used: _____
_____
_____

How the other person exhibited the behavior: _____
_____
_____

How you paced the behavior: _____
_____
_____

Results: _____
_____
_____

EXERCISE #12 — CROSS OVER MIRRORING

RESPONSES

Behavior the other person used: _____
_____
_____

Behavior you used: _____
_____
_____

How the other person exhibited the behavior: _____
_____
_____

How you paced the behavior: _____
_____
_____

Results: _____
_____
_____

EXERCISE #13
PACING & LEADING—1

INSTRUCTIONS

Pick a behavior from the list. Observe how another person uses the behavior. Use either mirroring or cross-over mirroring to pace the other person. Alter your own pacing behavior and observe the other person's behavior change. Repeat the exercise until you like the results you get. Then describe what you did and the results you got on the next page.

EXAMPLE:

#1 Mirroring: You observe that the other person is using mostly kinesthetic predicates. *You respond by using kinesthetic predicates* (pacing) *Gradually, you begin to introduce more and more auditory digital predicates to your responses* (leading). *You observe the other person's response.*

#2 Cross-over mirroring: You observe that the other person is breathing very slowly. *You move your index finger slowly, matching the rhythm of the breathing* (pacing). *Gradually, you quicken the movement of your finger* (leading). *You observe the other person's breathing change.*

NOTE: Changing your pacing behavior such that the other person's behavior also changes is called leading.

EXERCISE #13
PACING AND LEADING-1

RESPONSES

Behavior the other person used:_____
_____
_____

How the other person exhibited the behavior: _____
_____
_____

Did you use mirroring or cross-over mirroring?_____
_____
_____

How you paced the other person: _____
_____
_____

How you changed your own behavior to lead the other person: _____
_____
_____

Results Pacing:_____
_____
_____

Results Leading:_____
_____
_____

EXERCISE #13
PACING AND LEADING-1

RESPONSES

Behavior the other person used:_____
_____
_____

How the other person exhibited the behavior: _____
_____
_____

Did you use mirroring or cross-over mirroring?_____
_____
_____

How you paced the other person: _____
_____
_____

How you changed your own behavior to lead the other person: ____
_____
_____

Results Pacing:_____
_____
_____

Results Leading:_____
_____
_____

EXERCISE #14
PACING & LEADING—2

INSTRUCTIONS

Observe another person. Use any methods you have learned to determine the preferred representational system that person is using at the time you are observing him/her. Pace as many of the behaviors as you can in any of the ways you have learned. Change as many of your behaviors as you need to lead the other person into another representational system. When you like the result you get, describe what you did and the results on the next page.

EXAMPLE:

You observe that the other person is using visual accessing cues, visual predicates and is breathing rapidly and high in the chest. *You pace the breathing by rocking your body to the rhythm of the breathing and use the visual predicates in your responses. As you begin to slow the movement of your body you also begin adding some kinesthetic predicates to your responses. You observe the corresponding changes in the other person's behavior.*

EXERCISE #14
PACING AND LEADING—2

RESPONSES

Preferred representational system you believe the other person used: _____
_____
_____   _____

Behaviors the other person used:_____
_____
_____

How you paced the behaviors: _____
_____
_____

How you changed your behavior to lead: _____
_____
_____

Results Pacing:_____
_____
_____

Results Leading:_____
_____   _____
_____

EXERCISE #14
PACING AND LEADING—2

RESPONSES

Preferred representational system you believe the other person used: _____
_____
_____

Behaviors the other person used:_____
_____
_____

How you paced the behaviors: _____
_____
_____

How you changed your behavior to lead: _____
_____
_____

Results Pacing:_____
_____
_____

Results Leading:_____
_____
_____

SUGGESTED EXERCISES
PACING AND LEADING

GROUP EXERCISE

Participants: Person A - observer
Person B - speaker
Person C - leader

Procedure:
"A" and "C" identify a particular behavior that "C" will pace and lead. This can be any observable behavior such as "B's" breathing rate, minimal hand gestures, posture or blink rate. "B" sits facing "C" and begins to talk about anything of interest. "C" simply listens while pacing the chosen behavior (using mirroring or cross-over mirroring), then leads. The observer notes the success of the leading interaction by identifying a change in the specified behavior. Repeat the exercise until all have had a chance to be "leader".

INDIVIDUAL EXERCISE

Procedure:
A restaurant is an excellent setting for this exercise. Observe the interactions of individuals seated around you. Notice which individuals are pacing and how often they lead. *(NOTE: Be aware that pacing and leading will be taking place outside the conscious awareness of the individuals involved).* Pay attention to interactions that you would characterize as representing good rapport and to interactions in which there appears to be conflict. What is the difference in the pacing behaviors between the two?

ANCHORING

These exercises have been designed to help you recognize naturally occuring anchors and to use intentional and unintentional anchors.

ANCHORING: SOURCE MATERIAL

1   **Neuro-Linguistic Programming, Vol. I,** Dilts, Grinder, Bandler, Bandler, and DeLozier, Meta Publications, 1980; pp. 119-151, 223-227

2   **Frogs Into Princes,** Bandler and Grinder, Real People Press, 1979; pp. 79-136

3   **Solutions,** Cameron-Bandler, Real People Press, 1978; pp. 107-125.

ANCHORING CONTENT REVIEW

1. Define:
   a. Intentional Cueing _____
   b. Anchoring _____
   c. Stimulus _____
   d. Response _____
   e. Cues _____
   f. Naturally Occuring Anchors _____

2. The process of intentional anchoring involves:

   a. Exquisite timing

   b. The intentional cueing of internal resources

   c. S-R behaviors

   d. All of the above

3. How long does an anchor need to be held? _____
   _____

4. How often do anchors need to be repeated? _____
   _____

5. Can anchoring be used within a person's conscious awareness?
   _____

6. Can anchoring be done in any of the sensory systems? _____
   _____

7. How do you know when an anchor is successfully installed? ____
   _____

EXERCISE #15
RECOGNIZING ANCHORS

INSTRUCTIONS

On the following page is a list of things that are anchors for some people. Determine in what representational system each anchor operates. Enter the appropriate code in the space provided.

CODE

A-AUDITORY TONAL   K-KINESTHETIC

V-VISUAL   O/G-OLFACTORY GUSTATORY

EXAMPLE:

Someone Frowns   _V_

NOTE: Some may be anchors in more than one system.

EXERCISE #15 — RECOGNIZING ANCHORS

RESPONSES

_____Waving

_____Cough

_____Smell of Chicken Frying

_____Fingernails on
      Blackboard

_____Food on a Plate

_____Smile

_____Doubled Fist

_____Chair Seat

_____Itch

_____Untied Shoelace

_____Factory Whistle

_____Cigarette Smoke

_____Telephone Ringing

_____Perfume

_____Door Slams

_____Lawnmower Motor

_____Alarm Clock Ringing

_____Handshake

_____Hand on your arm

_____Pillow against the head

_____Sneeze

_____Coffee Perking

_____Newspaper Advertisement

_____Television Advertisement

What would be an example of an auditory digital anchor?

_____

EXERCISE #15 — RECOGNIZING ANCHORS

RESPONSES

_____Waving	_____Telephone Ringing
_____Cough	_____Perfume
_____Smell of Chicken Frying	_____Door Slams
_____Fingernails on Blackboard	_____Lawnmower Motor
_____Food on a Plate	_____Alarm Clock Ringing
_____Smile	_____Handshake
_____Doubled Fist	_____Hand on your arm
_____Chair Seat	_____Pillow against the head
_____Itch	_____Sneeze
_____Untied Shoelace	_____Coffee Perking
_____Factory Whistle	_____Newspaper Advertisement
_____Cigarette Smoke	_____Television Advertisement

What would be an example of an auditory digital anchor?

_____

EXERCISE #16
NATURALLY OCCURING ANCHORS

INSTRUCTIONS

In the next few days, become aware of the anchors that occur for you in your home, work or other environments. Include specific things that you do or say that elicit a particular response from other people as well as those that get a response from you. List each of the anchors in the spaces provided on the next page. Then code each of them, indicating the representational system in which each of them occurs. (Use the same code as in the previous exercise and add *Ad* for auditory digital).

EXAMPLE:

ANCHOR	RESPONSE	REPRESENTATIONAL SYSTEM
phone rings	answer it	A
car horn honks	gets attention	A
wave	wave back	V
handed a note	read it	V/Ad
kiss	kiss back	K

EXERCISE #16
NATURALLY OCCURING ANCHORS

RESPONSES

ANCHOR	RESPONSE	REPRESENTATIONAL SYSTEM

EXERCISE #16
NATURALLY OCCURING ANCHORS

RESPONSES

ANCHOR	RESPONSE	REPRESENTATIONAL SYSTEM

EXERCISE #17
ANCHORING

INSTRUCTIONS

Observe another person until you have calibrated to a particular internal state of that person. Anchor that state using any representational system you choose. Wait for at least ten minutes (or until you no longer observe the minimal cues associated with the state to which you calibrated). Fire the anchor. Observe what happens. Repeat the exercise until you like the response you get. When you are satisfied with the response, choose another system and anchor using that system. Repeat the exercise until you have anchored in the visual, auditory and kinesthetic systems.

EXAMPLE:

You observe someone frowning and describing an unpleasant encounter with an individual. *You anchor that state by sighing loudly. Ten minutes later, as you are discussing something else, you sigh loudly again (the same way you did it before). You observe the changes in the other person.*

EXERCISE #17 ANCHORING

RESPONSES

Internal state you calibrated: _____
_____

External behaviors that indicated the state: _____
_____
_____

Anchor you used:_____

System in which you anchored: _____

Results: _____
_____
_____

Internal state you calibrated: _____
_____

External behaviors that indicated the state: _____
_____
_____

Anchor you used:_____

System in which you anchored: _____

Results: _____
_____
_____

EXERCISE #17 Cont'd

Internal state you calibrated: _____

_____

External behaviors that indicated that state:_____

_____

_____

Anchor you used:_____

System in which you anchored: _____

Results: _____

_____

_____

_____

EXERCISE #17 ANCHORING

RESPONSES

Internal state you calibrated: _____

_____

External behaviors that indicated the state: _____

_____

_____

Anchor you used: _____

System in which you anchored: _____

Results: _____

_____

_____

Internal state you calibrated: _____

_____

External behaviors that indicated the state: _____

_____

_____

Anchor you used: _____

System in which you anchored: _____

Results: _____

_____

_____

EXERCISE #17 Cont'd

Internal state you calibrated: _____

_____

External behaviors that indicated that state:_____

_____

_____

Anchor you used:_____

System in which you anchored: _____

Results: _____

_____

_____

_____

SUGGESTED EXERCISES
ANCHORING

GROUP EXERCISE

Participants: Person A - facilitates

Person B - experiences

Procedure:

"A" and "B" face each other. "B" thinks of some very positive, happy, enthusiastic experience. As "B" does this, "A" calibrates to this internal state. When "A" has finished calibrating, "B" gives "A" one word that maximally represents that particular state for "B". When "B" says the word (s)he should use a tone of voice that also maximally represents the experience. "A" listens to the word and repeats it back using exactly the same intonation that "B" used. "A" may practice a few times using "B" as a coach. As soon as "A" can reproduce the word to "B's" satisfaction, "B" thinks about some aspect of his/her personal life where (s)he is not completely satisfied, some place where (s)he is "blocked", inhibited, or experiencing a lack of choice. When "B" is completely absorbed in the experience, (s)he signals with a nod. "A" then says the cue word for the positive experience and observes "B's" minimal cues as they change in response to this stimulus.

This is an exciting exercise to watch. It can also be run with groups of three with the third member as an "observer". After the exercise is completed "B" reports on his/her experience hearing the cue word. Then rotate positions and repeat the exercise.

INDIVIDUAL EXERCISE

Procedure:

Identify for yourself a situation you have experienced in which you exhibited specific qualities that you liked such as calmness, poise, resourcefulness, etc. Choose a specific word that embodies the experience. Say it to yourself, practicing until it becomes easy and automatic. The next time you are in a position where you need to have the qualities represented by the word, simply say it to yourself.

THE META-MODEL

These exercises have been designed to help you sharpen your ability to recognize and challenge Meta-Model violations.

THE META-MODEL: SOURCE MATERIAL

1 **Magic of NLP Demystified,** Lewis and Pucelik, Metamorphous Press, 1982; pp. 68-110.

META-MODEL
CONTENT REVIEW

1. Define:
   a. Generalization _____
   b. Cause and effect_____
   c. Complex equivalent _____
   d. Deletion_____
   e. Deep structure_____
   f. Lost performative _____
   g. Mind reading _____
   h. Modal operator of necessity _____
   i. Modal operator of possibility_____
   j. Nominalization _____
   k. Generalized referential index _____
   l. Reversed referential index_____
   m. Surface Structure _____
   n. Distortion_____
   o. Universal quantifier_____
   p. Unspecified verb_____

2. What are the three categories of the Meta-Model? _____
   _____,_____ and_____

3. How does challenging a person's Meta-Model violations help
   to expand his/her model of the world? _____
   _____

4. A nominalization is a _____that has been
   changed into a _____.

5. An assumption is an example of which of the universal human modeling processes?_____

6. The Meta-Model is used to:
   a. Gather information
   b. Identify limits to a person's model of the world
   c. Expand a person's limitations
   d. Provide a person with more choices about how to experience the world
   e. All of the above

EXERCISE #18
CHALLENGING
META-MODEL VIOLATIONS

INSTRUCTIONS

For each of the types of Meta-Model violations listed on the following pages, first give an example and then an appropriate challenge for that violation.

EXAMPLE:

DELETED REFERENTIAL INDEX: *John did.*

CHALLENGE: *John did what?*

EXERCISE #18
CHALLENGING META—MODEL VIOLATIONS

RESPONSES

GATHERING INFORMATION

Deleted Referential Index: _____

Challenge: _____

Unspecified Referential Index: _____

Challenge _____

Generalized Referential Index _____

Challenge: _____

Reversed Referential Index: _____

Challenge: _____

Nominalization: _____

Challenge: _____

Unspecified Verb: _____

Challenge: _____

EXERCISE #18 Cont'd

EXPANDING LIMITS:

Modal Operators of Necessity: _____

Challenge: _____

Modal Operators of Possibility: _____

Challenge: _____

Universal Quantifiers: _____

Challenge: _____

CHANGING MEANINGS

Cause and Effect: _____

Challenge: _____

Mind Reading: _____

Challenge: _____

Projected Mind Reading: _____

Challenge: _____

Lost Performative: _____

Challenge: _____

EXERCISE #18
CHALLENGING META—MODEL VIOLATIONS

RESPONSES

GATHERING INFORMATION

Deleted Referential Index: _____

Challenge: _____

Unspecified Referential Index: _____

Challenge: _____

Generalized Referential Index: _____

Challenge: _____

Reversed Referential Index: _____

Challenge: _____

Nominalization: _____

Challenge: _____

Unspecified Verb: _____

Challenge: _____

EXERCISE #18 Cont'd
EXPANDING LIMITS:

Modal Operators of Necessity: _____

Challenge: _____

Modal Operators of Possibility: _____

Challenge: _____

Universal Quantifiers: _____

Challenge: _____

CHANGING MEANINGS

Cause and Effect: _____

Challenge: _____

Mind Reading: _____

Challenge: _____

Projected Mind Reading: _____

Challenge: _____

Lost Performative: _____

Challenge: _____

EXERCISE #19 HEARING META—MODEL VIOLATIONS

INSTRUCTIONS

For this exercise use the tape. You will hear ninety sentences. Each sentence contains at least one Meta-Model violation. Each sentence will be followed by a pause. After you have heard the sentence, record the Meta-Model violation you heard. (Use the code below). When you have finished, go back and listen to the tape again. This time write an appropriate challenge for each Meta-Model violation you hear.

CODE

D	DELETED REFERENTIAL INDEX
U	UNSPECIFIED REFERENTIAL INDEX
G	GENERALIZED REFERENTIAL INDEX
R	REVERSED REFERENTIAL INDEX
N	NOMINALIZATION
UV	UNSPECIFIED VERB
MON	MODAL OPERATOR OF NECCESSITY
MOP	MODAL OPERATOR OF POSSIBILITY
UQ	UNIVERSAL QUANTIFIER
MR	MIND READING
PMR	PROJECTED MIND READING
CE	CAUSE AND EFFECT
LP	LOST PERFORMATIVE

EXAMPLE:

You hear: "John did it!"

META—MODEL VIOLATION	CHALLENGE
URI	*John did what?*

102

EXERCISE #19 HEARING META—MODEL VIOLATIONS

RESPONSES

VIOLATION	CHALLENGE
1.	
2.	
3.	
4.	
5.	
6.	
7.	
8.	
9.	
10.	
11.	
12.	
13.	
14.	
15.	
16.	
17.	
18.	
19.	
20.	
21.	
22.	
23.	
24.	
25.	
26.	
27.	
28.	
29.	
30.	

EXERCISE #19 Cont'd

VIOLATION	CHALLENGE
31.	
32.	
33.	
34.	
35.	
36.	
37.	
38.	
39.	
40.	
41.	
42.	
43.	
44.	
45.	
46.	
47.	
48.	
49.	
50.	
51.	
52.	
53.	
54.	
55.	
56.	
57.	
58.	
59.	
60.	

EXERCISE #19 Cont'd

VIOLATION	CHALLENGE
61.	
62.	
63.	
64.	
65.	
66.	
67.	
68.	
69.	
70.	
71.	
72.	
73.	
74.	
75.	
76.	
77.	
78.	
79.	
80.	
81.	
82.	
83.	
84.	
85.	
86.	
87.	
88.	
89.	
90.	

EXERCISE #19 HEARING META—MODEL VIOLATIONS

RESPONSES

VIOLATION	CHALLENGE
1.	
2.	
3.	
4.	
5.	
6.	
7.	
8.	
9.	
10.	
11.	
12.	
13.	
14.	
15.	
16.	
17.	
18.	
19.	
20.	
21.	
22.	
23.	
24.	
25.	
26.	
27.	
28.	
29.	
30.	

EXERCISE #19 Cont'd

VIOLATION	CHALLENGE
31.	
32.	
33.	
34.	
35.	
36.	
37.	
38.	
39.	
40.	
41.	
42.	
43.	
44.	
45.	
46.	
47.	
48.	
49.	
50.	
51.	
52.	
53.	
54.	
55.	
56.	
57.	
58.	
59.	
60.	

EXERCISE #19 Cont'd

VIOLATION	CHALLENGE
61.	
62.	
63.	
64.	
65.	
66.	
67.	
68.	
69.	
70.	
71.	
72.	
73.	
74.	
75.	
76.	
77.	
78.	
79.	
80.	
81.	
82.	
83.	
84.	
85.	
86.	
87.	
88.	
89.	
90.	

EXERCISE #20
SEEING META-MODEL
VIOLATIONS

INSTRUCTIONS

Some of the sentences in the following article contain Meta-Model violations. Some of them will contain more than one violation. Go through the article sentence by sentence. Above the place where it occurs in the sentence, code each Meta-Model violation (using the code you used for exercise #19). The first sentence has been done for you as the example.

EXAMPLE

    GRI   URI
Teachers do it.

EXERCISE #20
SEEING META—MODEL VIOLATIONS

RESPONSES

"Teachers do it. Veterinarians do it. So do therapists and people who sell real estate."

A new system of communication that goes by the unwieldy name of Neuro-Linguistic Programming is the band-wagon being jumped upon by a lot of people who deal with other people.

Their battle cry: "The communication is the response." (Translation: It's not what you say or how you say it but how it affects the other guy that matters.)

Their gurus: Richard Bandler and John Grinder. two social scientists who came up with the idea of Neuro-Linguistic Programming in the mid-1970s. They got the idea by closely observing successful communicators. and they found that those people did not operate solely on a verbal plane. There is a lot more to talking than speech. and Grinder and Bandler developed a system for teaching people this more fruitful form of communicating.

Say you "communicate" something. How do you know if the reponse you get is the one you seek. Not in so many words. Neuro-Linguistic Programming employs body language of a very sophisticated type. Practitioners are taught to watch for changes in skin tone or color, dilations of pupils, flaring of nostrils, the slightest hint of muscle tension or delicate changes in breathing patterns.

Sound difficult? Grinder and Bandler say it's not. They insist that learning to see such minor changes is a learned response and that any person, with proper application, can become an expert observer.

The best place to start observing, they say, is with the eyes.

Ask someone what color shoes his kindergarten teacher wore. Watch his face carefully. The eyes will probably make a quick darting movement up and to his left (your right) as he "accesses" a remembered image.

Ask him to think about the melody of "Bette Davis Eyes." The eyes will go directly to his left as he remembers sounds. If you ask for a "constructed" sound, one that he has to make up--say, the sound of a spider might make while it walks--the eyes will slide to his right and back.

A request for a feeling or smell or taste (what does fur feel like?) will send the eyes down and to his right. And so forth.

What do all these eye movements mean? Grinder and Bandler say they're just a trick, a way to get people to pay attention to their experiences, to learn to notice nuances. And nothing is graven in stone, they note. The usual eye movements may be reversed from left to right in left-handed people, or even in some right handers. All generalizations, they observe, are lies."

Reprinted with permission from "The Oregonian". March 15, 1982; Portland, Oregon. Article entitled: "What's That You Say? Eyes Have the Answer", by Frances M. Gardner.

112

EXERCISE #20
SEEING META—MODEL VIOLATIONS

RESPONSES

"Teachers do it. Veterinarians do it. So do therapists and people who sell real estate."

A new system of communication that goes by the unwieldy name of Neuro-Linguistic Programming is the band-wagon being jumped upon by a lot of people who deal with other people.

Their battle cry: "The communication is the response." (Translation: It's not what you say or how you say it but how it affects the other guy that matters.)

Their gurus: Richard Bandler and John Grinder, two social scientists who came up with the idea of Neuro-Linguistic Programming in the mid-1970s. They got the idea by closely observing successful communicators, and they found that those people did not operate solely on a verbal plane. There is a lot more to talking than speech, and Grinder and Bandler developed a system for teaching people this more fruitful form of communicating.

Say you "communicate" something. How do you know if the reponse you get is the one you seek. Not in so many words. Neuro-Linguistic Programming employs body language of a very sophisticated type. Practitioners are taught to watch for changes in skin tone or color, dilations of pupils, flaring of nostrils, the slightest hint of muscle tension or delicate changes in breathing patterns.

Sound difficult? Grinder and Bandler say it's not. They insist that learning to see such minor changes is a learned response and that any person, with proper application, can become an expert observer.

The best place to start observing, they say, is with the eyes.

Ask someone what color shoes his kindergarten teacher wore. Watch his face carefully. The eyes will probably make a quick darting movement up and to his left (your right) as he "accesses" a remembered image.

Ask him to think about the melody of "Bette Davis Eyes." The eyes will go directly to his left as he remembers sounds. If you ask for a "constructed" sound, one that he has to make up--say, the sound of a spider might make while it walks--the eyes will slide to his right and back.

114

A request for a feeling or smell or taste (what does fur feel like?) will send the eyes down and to his right. And so forth.

What do all these eye movements mean? Grinder and Bandler say they're just a trick, a way to get people to pay attention to their experiences, to learn to notice nuances. And nothing is graven in stone, they note. The usual eye movements may be reversed from left to right in left-handed people, or even in some right handers. All generalizations, they observe, are lies."

Reprinted with permission from "The Oregonian", March 15, 1982; Portland, Oregon. Article entitled: "What's That You Say? Eyes Have the Answer"; by Frances M. Gardner.

SUGGESTED EXERCISES
THE META-MODEL

GROUP EXERCISE

Participants: Person A - speaker
Person B - Meta-Modeler I
Person C - Meta-Modeler II

Procedure:
"A" begins by talking about anything of interest. "B" responds by challenging "A's" Meta-Model violations. When "B" gets stuck or tired (s)he tags "C" who takes "B's" place as Meta-Modeler. "B" and "C" may exchange tags any time they get stuck. After a prearranged time, "A" then shares his/her experience with "B" and "C". Rotate the positions until all have had an opportunity to be in the "A" position. Each round of the exercise can be limited to 5 or 10 minutes.

NOTE:
One goal of this exercise can be to challenge violations vigorously and maintain rapport with "A", thus preventing the tendency for the Meta-Modeler to become a "Meta-Monster".

INDIVIDUAL EXERCISE

Procedure:
Choose one of the Meta-Model violations to concentrate on for a week. During any conversation, while watching television, listening to the radio, or reading a book or newspaper, identify the Meta-Model violation whenever it occurs. Rehearse internally the appropriate challenge. Practice saying it out loud whenever it is appropriate. After one week choose another violation, concentrate on it for a week and forget the previous one, allowing it to slip into your unconscious where it will stay handy until you need it.

REFRAMING

These exercises have been designed to help you sharpen your ability to use reframing techniques.

REFRAMING: SOURCE MATERIAL

1   **Solutions,** Cameron-Bandler, Meta Publications, 1978; pp. 129-132.

2   **TRANCE-Formations,** Bandler and Grinder, Real People Press, 1981; pp. 137-177.

3   **Reframing,** Bandler and Grinder, Real People Press, 1982; entire.

4   **Precision,** McMaster and Grinder, Precision Models, 1980; pp. 35-105.

REFRAMING CONTENT REVIEW

1. Define:
   a. Simple reframe _____
   b. Outcome frame _____
   c. Models of the world _____

2. Reframing assumes that all behaviors are useful and appropriate in some context.   True or False

3. Emphasis on the positive value of any behavior can transform a potentially negative situation into a growing or learning experience.   True or False

4. When is a reframe useful?_____

5. How do you know that a reframe has been successful? _____
   _____

6. What are the six steps in the "six-step reframing procedure"?
   1. _____
   2. _____
   3. _____
   4. _____
   5. _____
   6. _____

EXERCISE #21
SIMPLE REFRAMES

INSTRUCTIONS

Respond to each of the statements on the following page with a simple reframe.

EXAMPLE:

These exercises are boring. *You must be good at them.*

EXERCISE #21 SIMPLE REFRAMES

RESPONSES

My Mother is a busybody. _____

_____

My husband works so hard that he doesn't have time to play with the
kids. _____

Someone shot and wounded the pope. _____

_____

When I figured my income tax this year, I owed the government
$2,000.00. _____

My daughter never shuts up. _____

_____

I just feel depressed all the time. _____

_____

My boss doesn't understand me. _____

_____

I am a bigot. _____

_____

Just when I begin to feel successful, I blow it. _____

_____

My husband never listens to me. _____

_____

EXERCISE #21 SIMPLE REFRAMES

RESPONSES

My Mother is a busybody. _____
_____

My husband works so hard that he doesn't have time to play with the kids._____

Someone shot and wounded the pope. _____
_____

When I figured my income tax this year, I owed the government $2,000.00_____

My daughter never shuts up._____
_____

I just feel depressed all the time. _____
_____

My boss doesn't understand me. _____
_____

I am a bigot. _____
_____

Just when I begin to feel successful, I blow it._____
_____

My husband never listens to me. _____
_____

EXERCISE #22
OUTCOME   FRAMES

INSTRUCTIONS

On the following page you will find a series of outcome statements. Read each statement and decide if it is a well-formed outcome. If the outcome is well-formed, write "yes" in the space provided. If the outcome is not well-formed, rewrite the statement in such a way that it meets the well-formed conditions. Then write a question you might have asked to elicit the well-formed response.

EXAMPLE:

statement: I don't want to be fat any more.

response: *I want to be able to look at myself in the mirror and hear myself say, "Boy, you sure look great!"*

question: *How would you know if you got the outcome you want?*

EXERCISE #22   OUTCOME FRAMES

RESPONSES

1. I want to be successful.
response _____
question _____

2. I want to be able to drink and not pick up a cigarette.
response _____
question _____

3. I want to feel good about myself.
response _____
question _____

4. I want to live in a nice house and drive an expensive car.
response _____
question _____

5. I don't want to be depressed any more.
response _____
question _____

6. I want my boss to tell me that I've done a good job, when I have.
response _____
question _____

7. I want to learn how to tell my children that I love them.
response _____
question _____

8. I want to be happy.
response _____
question _____

EXERCISE #22   OUTCOME FRAMES

RESPONSES

1. I want to be successful.
response _____
question _____

2. I want to be able to drink and not pick up a cigarette.
response _____
question _____

3. I want to feel good about myself.
response _____
question _____

4. I want to live in a nice house and drive an expensive car.
response _____
question _____

5. I don't want to be depressed any more.
response _____
question _____

6. I want my boss to tell me that I've done a good job, when I have.
response _____
question _____

7. I want to learn how to tell my children that I love them.
response _____
question _____

8. I want to be happy.
response _____
question _____

EXERCISE #23
SIX-STEP REFRAMING

INSTRUCTIONS

Each step in the six-step reframe represents a choice point for the reframer. On the following page you will be given a desired outcome for each step in the reframe. Read the outcome statement and then generate three possible ways of eliciting that outcome. Record your answers in the space provided.

EXAMPLE:

Outcome: Identify the specific pattern to be changed.

a. What is it specifically that you want to do differently?
b. What is it that you want to change?
c. If you could, what would you do differently?

EXERCISE #23
SIX-STEP REFRAMING

RESPONSES

1. Identify the specific pattern to be changed.
   a. _____
   b. _____
   c. _____

2. Establish communication with the part responsible for the behavior pattern to be changed.
   a. _____
   b. _____
   c. _____

3. Separate the behavior from the intention of the responsible part.
   a. _____
   b. _____
   c. _____

4. Generate new behaviors to accomplish the positive function.
   a. _____
   b. _____
   c. _____

5. Have the part take responsibility for choosing any of the new behaviors in the appropriate context.
   a. _____
   b. _____
   c. _____

6. Ask the other parts if they object to any of the choices generated as new behaviors.
   a. _____
   b. _____
   c. _____

EXERCISE #23
SIX-STEP REFRAMING

RESPONSES

1. Identify the specific pattern to be changed.
   a. _____
   b. _____
   c. _____

2. Establish communication with the part responsible for the behavior pattern to be changed.
   a. _____
   b. _____
   c. _____

3. Separate the behavior from the intention of the responsible part.
   a. _____
   b. _____
   c. _____

4. Generate new behaviors to accomplish the positive function.
   a. _____
   b. _____
   c. _____

5. Have the part take responsibility for choosing any of the new behaviors in the appropriate context.
   a. _____
   b. _____
   c. _____

6. Ask the other parts if they object to any of the choices generated as new behaviors.
   a. _____
   b. _____
   c. _____

SUGGESTED EXERCISES
REFRAMING

GROUP EXERCISE

Participants: Person A - originator of problem
All others - reframers

Procedure:
"A" thinks of a problem statement that accurately represents some problem (s)he is experiencing. The other members of the group take turns reframing the problem statement. "A" responds to each reframe by indicating that it is or is not an acceptable reframe for him/her. The exercise continues until the problem has been successfully reframed. The exercise may be repeated until many or all of the group have had an opportunity to be "A".

INDIVIDUAL EXERCISE

Procedure:
For the next week as you watch television, listen to the radio or are engaged in conversation with someone, practice internally reframing any "negative" statements that you hear. Practice responding aloud when it is appropriate. The news is an excellent source of challenges for the reframer!

A SET OF POSSIBLE RESPONSES TO SOME OF THE EXERCISES

ACCESSING CUES CONTENT REVIEW

1. Define:
   a. Eidetic Images _visually remembered events._
   b. Constructed Images _visually created images._
   c. Internal Dialogue _internal commentary on present, past or future._
   d. Internally Generated Stimuli _internal events, or perceptions, sounds, feelings, thoughts, etc._
   e. Lead System _system used to gain access to information stored in any system._
   f. Occular Accessing Cues _eye movements._
   g. Pupil Response _dilation or constriction of pupils in response to internally generated stimuli._
   h. Reversed Accessing Cues _reversed schematic, common in left-handers._

2. How can you identify people's accessing cues when their eyes are closed? _by watching the eye movements under the lids._

3. The "telephone posture" indicates what kind of accessing? _auditory tonal or digital._

4. When are you most likely to find reversed accessing cues? _when the individual is left handed._

5. Is the information people "access" always in their conscious awareness? _no, often one or more systems may be out of consciousness._

6. In response to the question. "What did you do last night?". the person flares his/her nostrils and closes his/her eyes. This is an example of _olfactory/gustatory_ accessing.

7. Give an example of where accessing cues are important.
   When a person answers "I don't know" to the question: "_What is bothering you?" but accesses visually, it can suggest that some visual information is out of conscious awareness._

EXERCISE #1
ELICITING ACCESSING CUES

RESPONSES

QUESTIONS	EYE MOVEMENT	SYSTEM
What color was your mother's hair when you last saw her?		V^r
What would your Mother look like with green hair?		V^c
Can you recall the tune to your favorite song?		A^r
What would that song sound like with church bells in the background?		A^c
What does snow feel like?		K
What are you telling yourself right now?		A^i

EXERCISE #2 — OBSERVING ACCESSING CUES

RESPONSES

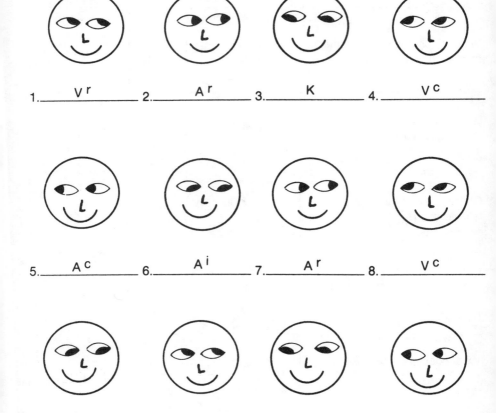

1. V^r 2. A^r 3. K   4. V^c

5. A^c 6. A^i 7. A^r 8. V^c

9. A^i 10. V^r 11. K   12. A^c

Exercise #2 Cont'd

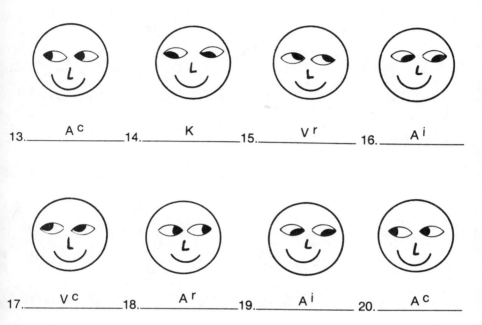

13. _____ A c _____ 14. _____ K _____ 15. _____ V r _____ 16. _____ A i _____

17. _____ V c _____ 18. _____ A r _____ 19. _____ A i _____ 20. _____ A c _____

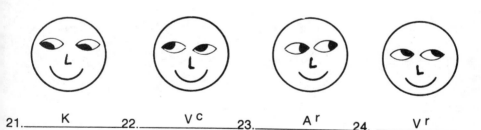

21. _____ K _____ 22. _____ V c _____ 23. _____ A r _____ 24. _____ V r _____

Exercise #2 Cont'd

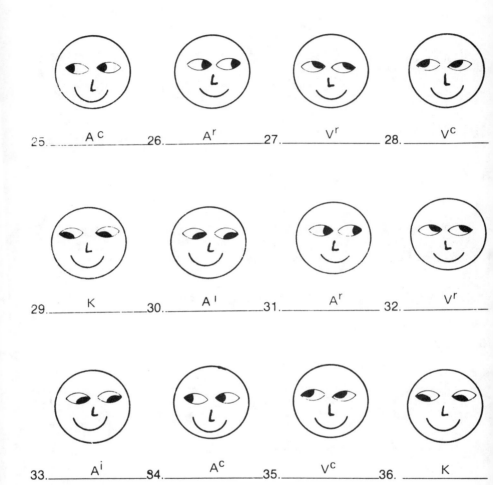

25. _____ A ^{c} 26. _____ A ^{r} 27. _____ V ^{r} 28. _____ V ^{c}

29. _____ K 30. _____ A ^{l} 31. _____ A ^{r} 32. _____ V ^{r}

33. _____ A ^{i} 34. _____ A ^{c} 35. _____ V ^{c} 36. _____ K

138

EXERCISE #3 — OBSERVING ACCESSING CUES

RESPONSES

  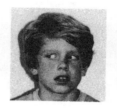 

1. _____ K _____   2. _____ V r _____   3. _____ A c _____   4. _____ A i _____

5. _____ V c _____   6. _____ A r _____   7. _____ V r _____   8. _____ V c _____

9. _____ A r _____   10. _____ K _____   11. _____ A i _____   12. _____ A c _____

Exercise #3 Cont'd

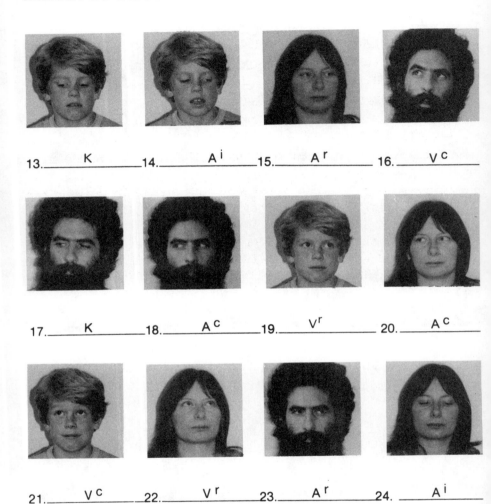

13.___K___ 14.___A ^{i}___ 15.___A ^{r}___ 16.___V ^{c}___

17.___K___ 18.___A ^{c}___ 19.___V ^{r}___ 20.___A ^{c}___

21.___V ^{c}___ 22.___V ^{r}___ 23.___A ^{r}___ 24.___A ^{i}___

CALIBRATION CONTENT REVIEW

1. Define:
    a. Calibration _identifying minimal cues associated with specific states._
    b. Minimal Cues _breathing patterns, skin tones, voice quality, posture, gestures, etc._
    c. Analog _any non-verbal communication._
    d. Calibrated Communication _(calibrated loops) a specific internal response that always occurs after a certain stimulus._
    e. Subliminal Cues _minimal cues outside of a person's awareness._

2. You know when you have calibrated to an individual when _you can recognize particular states whenever the person accesses them._

3. Name three situations in which the process of calibration can be useful.
   Sales - being able to calibrate a state of readiness to buy.
   Classroom - being able to judge when a student is ready to learn.
   Parenting - knowing when a child is disturbed about something.

4. Calibration is one way to demystify the apparent "mind reading" done by us all upon occasion. _True._

5. Calibration utilizes immediately verifiable sensory grounded experience to identify a person's _internal state._

EXERCISE #4   AUDITORY CALIBRATION

RESPONSES

PART ONE

KEY PHRASES AND TONALITIES

Sadness _feeling sick and helpless._

Happiness _I got all quivery inside._

Pleasure _so warm and comfortable._

Anger _I just hate it (emphasis on just)_

Defensiveness _You've got to understand...it's just that_

Excitement _absolutely thrilled (high pitched voice)_

Openess to learning _fascinates me... how do you do that?_

PART TWO

1. _Happy_	8. _Open to learning_	15. _Defensive_
2. _Pleasure_	9. _Happy_	16. _Pleasure_
3. _Anger_	10. _Defensive_	17. _Open to learning_
4. _Defensive_	11. _Pleasure_	18. _Excitement_
5. _Excitement_	12. _Happy_	19. _Anger_
6. _Open to learning_	13. _Anger_	20. _Sadness_
7. _Sadness_	14. _Sadness_	21. _Excitement_

EXERCISE #5 — VISUAL CALIBRATION

RESPONSES

1. _Anger_ 2. _Happiness_ 3. _Sadness_ 4. _Open to learning_

5. _Defensiveness_ 6. _Excitement_ 7. _Pleasure_ 8. _Happiness_

9. _Open to learning_ 10. _Anger_ 11. _Sadness_ 12. _Pleasure_

Exercise #5 Cont'd

   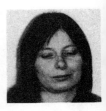

13. _Anger_   14. _Open to learning_   15. _Excitement_   16. _Pleasure_

17. _Happiness_   18. _Defensiveness_   19. _Sadness_   20. _Excitement_

21. _Anger_   22. _Pleasure_   23. _Defensiveness_   24. _Happiness_

PACING AND LEADING
CONTENT REVIEW

1. Define:
   a. Pacing _matching another's behavior(s) with your own._

   b. Leading _changing your behavior such that another also changes their behavior._

   c. Mirroring _matching a specific posture or gesture of another person._

   d. Rapport _sense of harmony or sympathy with another often the result of pacing._

   e. Predicates _verbs and adjectives and adverbs._

   f. Representational Systems _re-presentations of experience coded and stored in the brain (V, D, K, A, O/G)._

   g. Predicate Preference _habitual use of predicates from one representational system._

2. The word "understand" presupposes which representational system? _digital._

3. A person says in a monotone with arms folded over the chest, "I know what the potentialities are." This person is operating from which representational system? _digital._

4. You might expect a person who operates consistently from his/her emotions and feelings to use _kinesthetic_ predicates.

5. What is meant by the axiom, "pacing and leading are self perscriptive?" _you know to lead when the paced behavior increases and to return to pacing when the lead is no longer followed._

6. What are the primary ways of representing our experience? _visual, kinesthetic, auditory and digital._

145

7. How can a person's language indicate how (s)he makes sense of the world? *predicates describe the sensory experience of the speaker: such as feel, hear, think, smell, taste and see.*

8. What is the difference between a person's lead system and his/her preferred representational system? *the lead system is used to gain access to information that is usually stored in the preferred representational system.*

9. Give an example of mirroring in each of the following representational systems:

   VISUAL *matching the other person's gestures with the ones you use.*

   AUDITORY *matching the tone of another's voice with your own.*

   KINESTHETIC *using similar pressure to that received as when shaking hands.*

   DIGITAL *matching another's predicates when the ones they are using are from the digital system.*

146

EXERCISE #6 HEARING PREDICATES

RESPONSES

PREDICATES LIST:

characteristics
distinctions
regarding
representation
predispose
assume
digitalized
interpretation
rewarding
utterances
feel
flow
stumbling blocks
grab
feeling
excited

emotional
softer
deeper
sensitivity
emotions
resounding
arguments
attuning
tempo
discussion
listen
loud
quiet
ring
speech
cacophony

discussion
see
colorful
watching
gestures
perspectives
displayed
communicative
style
understand
tastefully
sour
taste
mouths
sweet
smell

EXERCISE #7
PACING REPRESENTATIONAL SYSTEMS

RESPONSES

VISUAL		KINESTHETIC		AUDITORY	
A	B	A	B	A	B
see	look	feel	touch	resounding	loud
colorful	vivid	flow	move	arguments	discussions
displayed	shown	stumbling blocks	bumps	attuning	hearing
gestures	pointed	grab	grasp	discussion	talking
perspectives	viewpoints	feeling	emotion	listen	hear
style	image	excited	joyous	loud	crash
		softer	gentler	quiet	silent
		deeper	lower	ring	bell
		sensitivity	emotive	talk	voluminous
		emotions	feelings	cacophony	speech
				discussion	speech
				communicative	talkative

EXERCISE #7
PACING REPRESENTATIONAL SYSTEMS

RESPONSES

AUDITORY DIGITAL		OLAFACTORY GUSTATORY	
A	B	A	B
characteristic	particular	tastefully	lip-smacking
distinction	variance	sour	salty
regarding	pertaining	taste	flavor
representation	model	mouths	lips
predispose	incline	sweet	sugary
assume	suppose	smell	aroma
digitalized	non-verbal		
interpretation	thought		
rewarding	response		
utterances	communications		
understand	know		

EXERCISE #9   HEARING VOICE CHANGES

RESPONSES

L↑ / L↑ / FN / ↓C / Q↓ / QM /

B↓ / ↓C / ↓Q / ↓Q / ↑B / ↓S /

↑N / ↑F / ↓Q / ↓S / ↑B / F /

F↑N / ↑L / ↓N / ↑N / ↓B / ↑F /

↓M / ↑BF / ↑C / ↓B / ↓S / BQ /

↓M / / / / / /

ANCHORING CONTENT REVIEW

1. Define:
   a. Intentional Cueing _using an established anchor._
   b. Anchoring _"attaching" a particular cue to an internal state or behavior._
   c. Stimulus _any cue that elicits a response._
   d. Response _an internal state or behavior elicited by an anchor_
   e. Cues _stimuli._
   f. Naturally Occuring Anchors _unintentional anchors._

2. The process of intentional anchoring involves:
   a. Exquisite timing
   b. The intentional cueing of internal resources
   c. S-R behaviors
   d. *All of the above*

3. How long does an anchor need to be held? _as long as it takes to ensure the stimulus response connection._

4. How often do anchors need to be repeated? _as often as necessary to ensure they remain installed._

5. Can anchoring be used within a person's conscious awareness? _yes._

6. Can anchoring be done in any of the sensory systems? _yes._

7. How do you know when an anchor is successfully installed? _when it elicits the desired response when fired._

EXERCISE #15 — RECOGNIZING ANCHORS

RESPONSES

V	Waving	A	Telephone Ringing
A	Cough	O/G	Perfume
O/G	Smell of Chicken Frying	A	Door Slams
A	Fingernails on Blackboard	A	Lawnmower Motor
V	Food on a Plate	A	Alarm Clock Ringing
V	Smile	K	Handshake
V	Doubled Fist	K	Hand on your arm
K	Chair Seat	K	Pillow against the head
K	Itch	K	Sneeze
V	Untied Shoelace	A/O/G	Coffee Perking
A	Factory Whistle	V	Newspaper Advertisement
O/G	Cigarette Smoke	V/A	Television Advertisement

What would be an example of an auditory digital anchor? $2 + 2 = 4$

META-MODEL CONTENT REVIEW

1. Define:
   a. Generalization _the ability to draw conclusions about a class from a particular._
   b. Cause and effect _the process of stimulus and response._
   c. Complex equivalent _words that are intangible and therefore defined differently by each individual._
   d. Deletion _leaving out information._
   e. Deep structure _the full representation of events._
   f. Lost performative _the evaluator is left out of the sentence._
   g. Mind reading _assuming you know what the other person thinks._
   h. Modal operator of necessity _words that require an action._
   i. Modal operator of possibility _words that exclude the possibility of a specific action._
   j. Nominalization _verbs that have been made into nouns._
   k. Generalized referential index _categories of people or events._
   l. Reversed referential index _reversing the receiver and actor._
   m. Surface Structure _spoken or written communication._
   n: Distortion _transforming perceptions or remembered experiences._
   o. Universal quantifier _generalizations that preclude exceptions_
   p. Unspecified verb _verbs that delete specifics of how. when. or where._

2. What are the three categories of the Meta-Model? _Gathering Information Expanding Limits, and Well Formed-Meanings._

3. How does challenging a person's Meta-Model violations help to expand his/her model of the world? _by reconnecting the person with perceptions and choices that may be outside the conscious awareness._

4. A nominalization is a _verb_ that has been changed into a _noun._

5. An assumption is an example of which of the universal human modeling processes? _generalization._

6. The Meta-Model is used to:
   a. Gather information
   b. Identify limits to a person's model of the world
   c. Expand a person's limitations
   d. Provide a person with more choices about how to experience the world
   e. *All of the above*

EXERCISE #18
CHALLENGING META—MODEL VIOLATIONS

RESPONSES

GATHERING INFORMATION

Deleted Referential Index: *John did.*

Challenge: *John did what?*

Unspecified Referential Index: *They are responsible for me.*

Challenge: *Who specifically is responsible for you?*

Generalized Referential Index: *Grown-ups are mean*

Challenge: *Which grown-ups specifically?*

Reversed Referential Index: *My mother hates me*

Challenge: *What is it about your Mother that you hate*

Nominalization: *This marriage isn't working*

Challenge: *What is it about being married that is a problem for you*

Unspecified Verb: *I love my kids*

Challenge: *How do you show your kids that you love them?*

EXERCISE #18 Cont'd
EXPANDING LIMITS:

Modal Operators of Necessity: *I have to go to work.*

Challenge: *What would happen if you didn't?*

Modal Operators of Possibility: *I can't do it.*

Challenge: *What stops you?*

Universal Quantifiers: *Nobody likes me.*

Challenge: *Can you think of one person who does?*

CHANGING MEANINGS

Cause and Effect: *He makes me hate him.*

Challenge: *How is his behavior causing you to hate him?*

Mind Reading: *He doesn't like me anymore.*

Challenge: *How do you know he doesn't like you?*

Projected Mind Reading: *He should know that I love him.*

Challenge: *How should he know that?*

Lost Performative: *Life is rough.*

Challenge: *According to whom?*

EXERCISE #19
HEARING META—MODEL VIOLATIONS

RESPONSES

VIOLATION		CHALLENGE
1.	MR	How do you know?
2.	SD	You don't mind what?
3.	GRI	Which cops?
4.	RRI	Why do you need your kids?
5.	UV	How does he pontificate?
6.	SD	Where is Spot running?
7.	UQ	*All* the time?
8.	LP	According to whom?
9.	N	How is convalescing dreary for you?
10.	MON	What would happen if you did?
11.	CE	How did your being there cause him to be upset?
12.	MOP	What stops you?
13.	MR	How do you know what she thinks?
14.	GRI	Which Russians are spies?
15.	PMR	How do they know that?
16.	MON	What would happen if you did?
17.	LP	According to whom?
18.	URI	What can you do?
19.	RRI	How do you nag Tom?
20.	UQ	*Always?*
21.	MOP	What stops you?
22.	N	How is relating a problem for you?
23.	SD	You did what?
24.	RRI	Why do you resent him?
25.	MON	What would happen if you didn't?
26.	PMR	How should I know that?
27.	CE	How did their actions force you?
28.	URI	Where did you go?
29.	GRI	Which teacher?
30.	SD	What can Pete teach?

EXERCISE #19 Cont'd

VIOLATION		CHALLENGE
31.	UV	How do my actions irritate you?
32.	MON	What would happen if you weren't?
33.	GRI	Which birds?
34.	N	How was encountering them favorable?
35.	RRI	Why don't you care about her?
36.	URI	What did she lose?
37.	UQ	Can you think of a time when I wasn't?
38.	CE	How did the devil make you do it?
39.	MR	How do you know he doesn't trust you?
40.	LP	According to whom?
41.	URI	Who are they?
42.	LP	According to whom?
43.	URI	What do you see?
44.	CE	What did you do to make her cry?
45.	N	How is living not fun for you?
46.	UV	How are you losing your mind?
47.	URI	What wasn't there?
48.	UQ	Everyone?
49.	MOP	What stops it from working?
50.	GRI	What books?
51.	RRI	Why do you hate them?
52.	MR	How do you know I'm not listening?
53.	LP	According to whom?
54.	CE	What does she do that makes you mad?
55.	URI	John can help whom?
56.	UV	How does he manipulate you?
57.	N	How are you obliged?
58.	GRI	Which men don't cry?
59.	MR	How do you know?
60.	SD	She lost what?

EXERCISE #19 Cont'd

VIOLATION		CHALLENGE
61. RRI	Why are you jealous of her?	
62. MON	What would happen if you didn't?	
63. PMR	How do you know that I know that?	
64. MOP	What stops you?	
65. GRI	Which people?	
66. MON	What would happen if you weren't?	
67. SD	Where did he run?	
68. UV	How is this program bugging you?	
69. UQ	**Everyone?**	
70. PMR	How do you know that she knows?	
71. NOP	What stops me?	
72. MR	How do you know what he thinks?	
73. UV	How am I procrastinating?	
74. UQ	Can you think of a time when she did?	
75. MOP	What stops you?	
76. UV	How is this exercise boring George?	
77. MON	What would happen if she weren't?	
78. PMR	How do you know he knows?	
79. CE	How did your actions cause her to leave?	
80. SD	You're not loved by whom?	
81. RRI	Try saying "I love my students."	
82. UQ	You've **never** done **anything** right, not once?	
83. PMR	How do you know I know?	
84. MR	How do you know that he doesn't love you?	
85. CE	How do your kids' actions drive you crazy?	
86. N	How is he not respecting you?	
87. LP	According to whom?	
88. UQ	**All** frogs have warts?	
89. MON	What will happen if I don't?	
90. LP/N/URI	How, what, when, where, and why do you know?!!	
UV/CE/MR		

EXERCISE #20
SEEING META—MODEL VIOLATIONS

RESPONSES

　　　GRI　　　　URI　　　GRI　　　　URI ┃ LP　URI　　　　URI　　　　　UV
"Teachers do it. Veterinarians do it. So do therapists and people who sell real

estate." DRI

LP　　　　　　　　　　　┃ N　　　　　　UV
A new system of communication that goes by the unwieldy name of Neuro-

　　　　　　　　　　　　　　　　　　　　　　　　　　CE　　　　　　　　　　GRI
Linguistic Programming is the band-wagon being jumped upon by a lot of people

　　　UV　　　　　GRI
who deal with other people.

　　URI　　　　　　　　　　　N　　　　　　　　　N　　DRI　　N
Their battle cry: "The communication is the response." (Translation: It's not what
　URI　　DRI　　　　　　URI　DRI　URI　CE　　　　　　　　　　　　　　　　DRI
you say or how you say it but how it affects the other guy that matters.)

　　URI　　　　　　　　　　　　　　　　　　　　　　　　　　　　　　　UV
Their gurus: Richard Bandler and John Grinder, two social scientists who came

up with the idea of Neuro-Linguistic Programming in the mid-1970s. They got the

　　　　　　　　　　　　　　　　　　　　　GRI
idea by closely observing successful communicators, and they found that those
　URI　　　　　　　UV　　　　　　　　　　　　　　LP　URI
people did not operate solely on a verbal plane. There is a lot more to talking than

　N　　　　　　　　　　　　　　　　　　　　　　　　　　　URI
speech, and Grinder and Bandler developed a system for teaching people this
　　　　　　　　　　N　　　　　　　　　DRI
more fruitful form of communicating.

160

Say you "communicate" something. How do you know if the reponse you get is the one you seek. Not in so many words. Neuro-Linguistic Programming employs body language of a very sophisticated type. Practitioners are taught to watch for changes in skin tone or color, dilations of pupils, flaring of nostrils, the slightest hint of muscle tension or delicate changes in breathing patterns.

Sound difficult? Grinder and Bandler say it's not. They insist that learning to see such minor changes is a learned response and that any person, with proper application, can become an expert observer.

The best place to start observing, they say, is with the eyes.

Ask someone what color shoes his kindergarten teacher wore. Watch his face carefully. The eyes will probably make a quick darting movement up and to his left (your right) as he "accesses" a remembered image.

Ask him to think about the melody of "Bette Davis Eyes." The eyes will go directly to his left as he remembers sounds. If you ask for a "constructed" sound, one that he has to make up--say, the sound of a spider might make while it walks--the eyes will slide to his right and back.

A request for a feeling or smell or taste (what does fur feel like?) will send the eyes down and to his right. And so forth.

What do all these eye movements mean? Grinder and Bandler say they're just a trick, a way to get people to pay attention to their experiences, to learn to notice nuances. And nothing is graven in stone, they note. The usual eye movements may be reversed from left to right in left-handed people, or even in some right handers. All generalizations, they observe, are lies."

Reprinted with permission from "The Oregonian", March 15, 1982, Portland, Oregon. Article entitled: "What's That You Say? Eyes Have the Answer", by Frances M. Gardner.

162

REFRAMING CONTENT REVIEW

1. Define:
   a. Simple reframe _changing a negative statement into a positive one._
   b. Outcome frame _well-formed goals._
   c. Models of the world _ways in which different people express different experiences of the world._

2. Reframing assumes that all behaviors are useful and appropriate in some context. _True._

3. Emphasis on the positive value of any behavior can transform a potentially negative situation into a growing or learning experience. _True._

4. When is a reframe useful? _when a person's representation of an experience is limited by a negative frame._

5. How do you know that a reframe has been successful? _when the person is willing to accept that the reframe is a valid representation of their experience._

6. What are the six steps in the "six-step reframing procedure"?
   1. _determine behavior to change_
   2. _establish communication with the responsible part_
   3. _separate the behavior from the positive intention_
   4. _generate three alternatives that get the positive outcome_
   5. _ask the part to take responsibility for choosing a new behavior in the appropriate context_
   6. _ecological check_

EXERCISE #21 SIMPLE REFRAMES

RESPONSES

My Mother is a busybody. *She must care a lot about other people.*

My husband works so hard that he doesn't have time to play with the kids. *He must want you to have a nice standard of living.*

Someone shot and wounded the pope. *It certainly brought the problems of terrorism to the attention of people worldwide.*

When I figured my income tax this year, I owed the government $2.000.00. *You must have made a lot more money last year than you did the year before.*

My daughter never shuts up. *She must be very bright to have so much to say.*

I just feel depressed all the time. *You certainly are in touch with your feelings.*

My boss doesn't understand me. *He is very lucky to have an employee who is so very different from himself.*

I am a bigot. *You must be very discerning.*

Just when I begin to feel successful, I blow it. *You are very self-perceptive.*

My husband never listens to me. *He's lucky you show him you love him in so many ways he doesn't need to hear you say it!*

EXERCISE #22   OUTCOME FRAMES

RESPONSES

1. I want to be successful.
response *I want to increase my salary to $40,000 per year*
question *How will you demonstrate your success to yourself and others?*

2. I want to be able to drink and not pick up a cigarette.
response *yes.*

3. I want to feel good about myself.
response *yes.*

4. I want to live in a nice house and drive an expensive car.
response *yes.*

5. I don't want to be depressed any more.
response *I want to feel happy more of the time.*
question *Since you don't want to be depressed, what do you want?*

6. I want my boss to tell me that I've done a good job, when I have.
response *I want to feel comfortable asking my boss to tell me if my work is good.*
question *How can you say that so you are the one controlling the outcome?*

7. I want to learn how to tell my children that I love them.
response *yes.*

8. I want to be happy.
response *I want to smile more often.*
question *How would you know if you are happy?*

EXERCISE #23   REFRAMING

RESPONSES

1. Identify the specific pattern to be changed.
a. *What would you like to be doing differently?*
b. *If you could imagine changing something about yourself, what would it be?*
c. *What behavior is it that you would change if you could?*

2. Establish communication with the part responsible for the behavior pattern to be changed.
a. *Go inside and ask the part if it is willing to communicate in consciousness.*
b. *Pay exquisite attention to your internal experience as you ask the part of you responsible for the behavior if it is willing to communicate with you.*
c. *Go inside and get in touch with the part of you that does x* and ask it if it is willing to communicate with you in consciousness.

3. Separate the behavior from the intention of the responsible part.
a. *Re-contact the part and ask it what it does for you by making you x?*
b. *Would you be willing to let me know what you are doing for me by x?*
c. *Ask the part if it is willing to let you know in consciousness what it does for you by causing you to do x.*

4. Generate new behaviors to accomplish the positive function.
a. *Ask the part if it is willing to generate three alternative ways to achieve the same thing.*
b. *Ask your creative part if it is willing to generate three ways that you could achieve the same outcome.*
c. *Ask your creative part to assist the part that does x in finding three new ways for you to get the same results.*

5. Have the part take responsibility for choosing any of the new behaviors in the appropriate context.
a. *Ask the part if it is willing to take responsibility for choosing one of the new behaviors in the future.*
b. *Tell the part that you thank it for what it does for you and ask it if it is willing to help you by choosing one of the new ways to get it.*
c. *Tell the part that it now has four ways of getting the result and ask it if in the future it would be willing to choose one of the new ways each time it is appropriate.*

6. Ask the other parts if they object to any of the choices generated as new behaviors.
a. *Have the part contact all your other parts and make sure they are ok with the new choices.*
b. *Go inside and ask your other parts if they object to any of the choices.*
c. *Ask your other parts if any of them have any problem with the new choices.*

Metamorphous Press

Metamorphous Press is a publisher and distributor of books and other media providing resources for personal growth and positive changes. MP publishes and distributes leading edge ideas that help people strengthen their unique talents and discover that we are responsible for our own realities.

Many of our titles center around NeuroLinguistic Programming (NLP). NLP is an exciting, practical, and powerful model of observable patterns of behavior and communication and the processes that underlie then.

Metamorphous Press provides selections in many useful subject areas such as communication, health and fitness, education, business and sales, therapy, women's interests, selections for young persons, and other subjects of general and specific interest. Our products are available in fine bookstores around the world. Among our distributors for North America are:

Baker & Taylor	Pacific Pipeline
Bookpeople	Inland Book Co.
New Leaf Distributors	Moving Books, Inc.

For those of you overseas, we are distributed by:
Airlift (UK, Western Europe)
Print World Ltd. (Indonesia)
Specialist Publications (Australia)

New selections are added regularly and availability and prices change, so ask for a current catalog or to be put on our mailing list. If you have difficulty finding our products in your favorite store, or if you prefer to order by mail, we will be happy to make our books and other products available to you directly. *Your interest and involvement with what we do is always welcome.* Please write or call us at:

METAMORPHOUS PRESS
P.O. Box 10616
Portland, Oregon 97210-0616
(503) 228-4972

TOLL FREE
1-800-937-7771

FAX (503) 223-9117

SKILL BUILDER SERIES

The **SKILL BUILDER SERIES** is a series of technique-building books covering all abilities from the beginner in NLP to the trainer. These manuals and workbooks will help you integrate and extend your knowledge gained through seminars or other books on NLP.

The Excellence Principle by Scout Lee, Ed.D. is a beginning manual filled with everything you need to get started with NLP. It was developed from Dr. Lee's notes written to present this exciting technology to the academic community. Filled with pictures, charts and diagrams to illustrate the concepts, this book will teach the reader skills in an amazing technology.
ISBN: 1-55552-003-0 Pbk.

Basic Techniques, Book I is a workbook designed for those who want to master the skills of NLP and for whom training is unavailable or not enough. This guidebook includes a set of practical, easy exercises you can do by yourself to integrate NLP skills you may learn in other books or seminars.
ISBN: 1-55552-016-2 Pbk.

Basic Techniques, Book II contains exercises a step further than Book I. Written for the reader who understands the essentials of NLP, this guidebook reinforces existing knowledge, provides clarification of terms, and gives step-by-step instructional exercises which can be done with two or more individuals. It is a valuable resource for those wishing to extend their skills in study groups.
ISBN: 1-55552-005-7 Pbk.

Your Balancing Act: Discovering New Life Through Five Dimensions of Wellness is the first of several planned workbooks of applied NLP technology, applied here to belief change in health and wellness. This workbook helps you to balance physical, emotional, social, mental and spiritual belief systems for optimum wellness.
ISBN: 0-943920-75-2 Pbk.

Advanced Techniques is designed as a reference for trainers. It is a collection of exercises of varying complexity detailed in the form of lesson plans. Information is provided with the intention of helping the leader of a group to assist the participants in getting maximum benefit from the exercises.
ISBN: 0-943920-08-6 Pbk.

The Challenge of Excellence applies NLP technology to leadership training. The "Challenge of Excellence" is an outdoor course of physical and emotional challenges on ropes, balance beams and poles where people test their limits and abilities--metaphors for the challenges of everyday life. Using NLP, this book shows the mind/body interconnection and our capacity for learning patterns of excellence.
ISBN: 1-55552-004-9 Pbk.

Get The Results You Want
Kim Kostere & Linda Malatesta
This book offers the knowledge and NLP skills necessary to make the process of personal change exciting and rewarding. It provides all people who work in innerpersonal communication and changework with a sound, step-by-step process for more effective results.
1-55552-015-4 Pbk.

POSITIVE
CHANGE
GUIDES

Magic of NLP Demystified
Byron Lewis & Frank Pucelik
This introductory NLP book gives readers a clear and understandable overview of the subject. It covers the basic concepts of NLP using "user-friendly" illustrations and graphics. One of the best introductory books available for new NLP students.
1-55552-017-0 Pbk.
0-943920-09-4 Cloth

Fitness Without Stress
Robert M. Rickover
This book explains the Alexander Technique, recognized today to be one of the most powerful methods of improving body movement and coordination as well as overall health. It is also a guide to finding an Alexander teacher. No previous experience necessary.
0-943920-32-9 Cloth

The Power of Balance
Brian W. Fahey, Ph.D.
The importance of balance in life is the emphasis of Fahey's book. It expands on the original ideas about balancing body structure, known as "Rolfing." Reading this thought-provoking text can be a step toward achieving high levels of energy and well-being.
0-943920-52-3 Cloth

These are only a few of the titles we offer. If you cannot find our books at your local bookstore, you can order directly from us. Call or write for free catalog information:

Metamorphous Press
P.O. Box 10616
Portland, Oregon 97210

Toll Free 1-800-937-7771
FAX 503-223-9117

Shipping and handling charges are $3.50 for each book and $.75 for each additional title. We ship UPS unless otherwise requested. Foreign orders please include $1 for each additional book . All orders must be prepaid in U.S. dollars. Please write or call directly to determine additional charges. Prices and availability may change without notice.

NOTES

NOTES

NOTES

NOTES

NOTES

NOTES

NOTES

NOTES